DWIGHT HOWARD

by John Fawaz

SCHOLASTIC INC.

New York   Toronto   London   Auckland
Sydney   Mexico City   New Delhi   Hong Kong

Photos:

Front cover and title page: NBAE/Getty images

Interior: NBAE/Getty Images (4, 6, 7, 14, 17, 18, 22, 23, 26, 28, 29, 30, 30-31); Getty Images (8, 20, 24, 32); WireImage/Getty Images (11, 12)

ISBN: 978-0-545-20646-4

12 11 10 9 8 7 6 5 4 3 2 1   10 11 12 13 14 15/0

Designed by Cheung Tai
Printed in the U.S.A.   40
First printing, January 2010

CONTENTS

CHAPTER 1 . . . . **5**

THE NEXT GREAT BIG MAN

CHAPTER 2 . . . . **9**

MR. BASKETBALL

CHAPTER 3 . . . . **15**

TAKING FLIGHT

CHAPTER 4 . . . . **21**

SUPERMAN

CHAPTER 5 . . . . **27**

GOOD AS GOLD

THE NEXT GREAT BIG MAN

In the 2009 NBA Playoffs, Dwight Howard made believers out of everyone.

"We believe we can win a championship. People used to laugh at me when I'd say that," Dwight said before Orlando played Cleveland in Game 6 of the Eastern Conference Finals. "But it's right there for us. We have a chance to take the next step."

That night, Dwight and the Magic took the next step by advancing to the NBA Finals with a 103-90 victory over the Cavaliers. He made 14 of 21 field goal attempts and 12 of 16 free throw attempts. He finished with 40 points and 14 rebounds.

"I don't think Dwight's ever played a more patient, under-control game than that one," Magic

Coach Stan Van Gundy said. "He made the right decision every time.

"I don't know what else he could have done today. He was fantastic. . . . He was unbelievable."

When his team needed him most, Dwight played his best. The 6-11 Howard stood ready to take his place as the NBA's next great big man.

But this is no ordinary big man. Dwight is one of the fastest players in the league and able to outrun many guards. He can handle the ball equally well with his left or right hand. His amazing leaping ability allows him sky above the rim. Strong, fast, athletic — and just 24 years old.

"For Dwight, it's all about work," Magic General Manager Otis Smith said. "He wanted to be great from day one, so he works hard at it. He's trying to be the best player to ever play. And even though he's had a good season, I think his best seasons are yet to come."

Dwight is already one of the most

popular players in the NBA. In 2009, he became the first player to receive 3 million fan votes for the NBA All-Star Game. He stays connected with his fans through his blog and social networking sites on the Internet. Dwight is often seen around town in Orlando, going to the movies or eating out. Then there is his smile. Dwight never leaves home without it.

Some say Dwight is too nice to be the greatest big man ever. He plans to prove them wrong.

"Basketball brings me joy and I'm having fun blocking shots and dunking, so I am going to smile," Dwight wrote on his blog. "I'm going to smile and have fun, but at the same time I'm still going to dunk on you."

MR. BASKETBALL

Dwight David Howard Jr. was born December 8, 1985, in Atlanta, Georgia to Dwight Howard Sr., a Georgia State Trooper, and Sheryl Howard, a teacher. Sheryl called Dwight a "miracle child" because she had been trying to have another child for eight years, since the birth of TaShanda, Dwight's older sister.

Dwight participated in many sports as a kid, but his favorites were basketball (he played guard) and baseball (he was a talented pitcher). He always had a smile on his face, whether he was singing in choir or horsing around with Jahaziel, his younger brother.

Dwight went to one school from kindergarten through 12th grade: Southwest Atlanta Christian Academy, where his mother taught and his father volunteered as Athletic Director. By age 12, Dwight had become quite a hoops player. He could handle the basketball equally well with his right or left hand, and he was a skilled passer who would rather share the ball than shoot it. His favorite NBA star was Michael Jordan.

At that time, Dwight began to think about his future. He wrote down eight life goals and taped the list over his bed. One of those goals: become the first player selected in the NBA Draft.

At the end of his freshman year of high school, Dwight broke his right leg. He healed quickly, and when he returned to the court a few months later, he had grown nearly half a foot, to 6-7. He continued growing, and soon he towered above everyone. His days as a guard were finished. Dwight had to learn a new position — center. Instead of imitating Jordan, now he tried to copy the moves of Kevin Garnett.

By his senior season, Dwight had developed into one of the best high school players in the nation. Southwest Atlanta Christian Academy was a small private school that had never enjoyed much sports success. Dwight changed all that, and fans packed the school's tiny gym to see him play. But all the attention did not change Dwight.

Like every student at Southwest Atlanta Christian

Academy, Dwight went to class wearing his school uniform. He arrived on campus driving an old car that his parents bought for $950. He began every day with prayer. Every night he had to do his homework and his chores, and of course, clean his room.

Dwight's parents made sure that no matter how high he soared on the court, he kept both feet on the ground outside the arena.

"My mom and dad really laid a great foundation for me about respect," Dwight said in 2009. "They always talked to me about respecting everybody . . . no matter what their status is in life. That's the way I grew up, always saying, 'Yes, sir,' or 'No, sir,' always trying to listen to my elders.

"It brought me a long way."

In 2004, Dwight led Southwest Atlanta Christian Academy to its first state title. He had a triple-double (26 points, 23 rebounds, and 10 blocked shots) in the championship game. He won several National High School Player of the Year Awards, and was named Georgia's "Mr. Basketball."

It seemed hard to believe that Dwight was just 18 years old. He was nearly seven feet tall, and he was very comfortable in the spotlight of television cameras and microphones thrust in front of him. Yet Dwight was still a kid at heart. He used the money his parents gave him for his 18th birthday to buy a DVD of his favorite movie (*Finding Nemo*), and then he watched it more than 100 times. With a smile nearly as broad as his shoulders, Mr. Basketball prepared to take the next step in his hoops journey.

TAKING FLIGHT

During Dwight Howard's senior season in high school, he was constantly asked if he would enter the 2004 NBA Draft. If he did, scouts predicted that he would be among the first 10 players drafted.

Dwight finally answered that question in April 2004, when he stood before a packed gym at Southwest Atlanta Christian Academy and announced his decision to play in the NBA. He told the crowd, "I will try to be a basketball player you will be proud to watch, and a young man you can be even prouder of."

After that, the only question became whether Dwight would be chosen first or second. The Orlando Magic, who had the first pick, said they would choose either Dwight or Emeka Okafor, a shot-blocking center from the University of Connecticut. The 21-year-old Okafor could help the Magic immediately. Dwight, on the other hand, probably needed to gain strength and experience.

Marty Blake, the long-time NBA Director of Scouting (he had been working in the League since the 1950s), said this about Dwight before the 2004 NBA Draft: "He's got great skills. Is he ready? I don't know. He wants to play. He works out every day. He gets up at five o'clock in the morning. He'll be a superstar . . . someday."

Dwight waited, like everyone else, to find out where he would be drafted — first by Orlando, or second by the Charlotte Bobcats. On June 24, 2004, NBA Commissioner David Stern stepped to the podium at Madison Square Garden in New York City and announced, "With the first pick in the 2004 NBA Draft, the Orlando Magic select Dwight Howard."

Dwight hugged his parents, shook hands with Okafor, and then went up to meet Stern. Dwight's dream of being the first player picked in the NBA Draft — one of eight goals he had written on a list taped above his bed when he was in ninth grade — had come true. Now it was time to get to work.

"I'm ready to play, ready to start the summer league, ready to run," he said on draft day.

Dwight certainly was ready. By the end of that summer, he had added nearly 25 pounds of muscle so he could stand firm against NBA centers. He also improved his shooting, footwork, and defense. The future was now for Dwight and the Orlando Magic.

Dwight made his NBA debut on November 3, 2004, when he played 38 minutes against the Milwaukee Bucks. He finished with 12 points, 10 rebounds, four blocked shots, and three steals. Dwight went on to start all 82 games, and he finished the season averaging 12.0 points, 10.0 rebounds, and 1.66 blocked shots per game. He became the first rookie since Shaquille O'Neal to record 10 or more rebounds in each of his first nine NBA games.

After the season, Dwight was a unanimous selection to the NBA All-Rookie First Team and finished third in the voting for the 2004-05 NBA Rookie of the Year Award. Most important, he helped the Magic improve their win-loss statistic to 36-46 in 2004-05 from 21-61 the season before.

Dwight had proven that he deserved to be the number-one pick. He had helped the Magic immediately, and he would only get better. The NBA's next great big man had taken flight. Now he was ready to soar.

CHAPTER 4

SUPERMAN

At the 2008 NBA Slam Dunk contest, Dwight Howard pulled off his Orlando Magic jersey to reveal a Superman shirt. After putting on a red cape, he raced toward the hoop, caught a pass in midair, and slammed it home. The crowd in New Orleans cheered wildly, as did former NBA greats Magic Johnson and Julius Erving, who were judging the contest.

Hello, world. Meet Dwight Howard, NBA superhero.

"It means a lot to me," Dwight said after winning the NBA Slam Dunk contest with 78 percent of the fan vote. "This one was really for the big men. People say big men don't look good dunking. I really wanted to win it for all the big men."

Most big men do not look good dunking, but

Dwight is no ordinary big man. He has the skills of a guard in his 6-11 frame, along with an amazing leaping ability (though not enough to leap tall buildings in a single bound). Combine that with his ear-to-ear smile and delightful personality, and the NBA had its newest star.

Dwight had been an excellent rebounder and defender almost from the day he joined the Magic in 2004. He soon developed into a potent offensive player, too. But early in his career, Dwight had been so determined to succeed as a player that he rarely showed his true self.

"In high school, I was in this small, little box, and then that box opened and I was released into the world," Dwight said. "It was hard at first — I was adjusting to playing all these games, learning how to interact with grown men."

Dwight received guidance from veteran teammates such as Steve Francis, Grant Hill, and Cuttino Mobley. On the court, they helped Dwight learn the game and improve as a player. Off the court, they helped him adjust to life as an

NBA player — the constant travel, managing his time, and avoiding all the distractions. One thing they all told Dwight: "Just be yourself."

"They really helped me out a lot," Dwight said in 2009. "Some things they taught me back then, I'm starting to realize right now. One of the things that really stood out to me was about my personality. When I first came into the League, I was a little quiet, shy. They would always tell me, 'You always

show us who you are, and your friends, but when you get in front of the media, you don't talk as much or smile, none of that.' They told me to bring out who I really was."

The "real" Dwight was a fun-loving kid at heart who loved to play hoops. His monster dunks and pure joy soon won over basketball fans around the world. Dwight's improvement as a player helped Orlando rise, too. He led the Magic to the NBA Playoffs in 2007, where they lost to Detroit in the First Round. The next season, Dwight was named to the 2007-08 All-NBA First Team after leading the League in rebounding (14.2 per game) and leading Orlando in scoring (20.7 points per game). The Magic finished with a 52-30 record and won the Southeast Division in the Eastern Conference.

In the 2008 NBA Playoffs, Orlando defeated Toronto in the First Round, the Magic's first win in a playoff series since 1996. Though Orlando's season ended with a loss to Detroit in the 2008 Eastern Conference Semifinals, the Magic's future looked bright. In just four seasons, Dwight had become one of the NBA's top players and had helped transform Orlando into a championship contender. Next stop: greatness.

CHAPTER 5

GOOD AS GOLD

After his summer trip to Beijing, China for the 2008 Summer Olympics, Dwight Howard entered the 2008-09 season more determined than ever to lead Orlando to an NBA championship.

"I'll carry the gold medal into our season," Howard said after he helped the USA Basketball team post an 8-0 record at the 2008 Summer Olympics. "My goal for the Magic is the same — win a gold. Oops, I mean a championship. If that's not the goal, then why are you playing?"

Dwight learned a lot during the Olympics, when he practiced with and played against the world's best players. He became more patient on offense and more focused on improving all parts of his game. He realized that his talent would only get him so far. He would have to work even harder to achieve his goals.

So Dwight pushed himself to become one of the NBA's most dominant players. He led the League in rebounding (13.8 per game) and blocked shots (2.9 per game) while ranking 18th overall in scoring (20.6 points per game). At 23, Dwight became the youngest basketball player ever to win the NBA Defensive Player of the Year Award. He also was named to the All-NBA First Team for the second consecutive season. But he had more work to do.

"I think we had a really good season, but we haven't accomplished anything yet," Howard said during the final week of the season.

Dwight knew that to be considered a great player he would have to lead his team to success in the playoffs. Though the Magic had won 59 games, hardly anyone gave them a chance to win the NBA title. LeBron James and the Cleveland Cavaliers were expected to represent the Eastern Conference in the 2009 NBA Finals, against Kobe Bryant and the Lakers. Kobe vs. LeBron was all anybody talked about.

But Dwight and the Magic had other ideas. Not only did Orlando win three playoff series to reach the NBA Finals, the Magic did it by overcoming several heart-breaking losses. In the First Round,

Orlando trailed Philadelphia two games to one after losing twice on last-second shots. But the Magic rallied to win three consecutive games.

In the Eastern Conference Semifinals, Orlando faced the Boston Celtics, who were trying to win their second straight NBA championship.

The Magic trailed three games to two, but they won Game 6 and then stunned everyone by winning Game 7 at Boston. Orlando followed that series with another upset, this time defeating LeBron and the Cavaliers in six games to advance to the NBA Finals. Kobe vs. LeBron? How about Kobe vs. Dwight?

Though Orlando lost to the Lakers in the NBA Finals, Dwight and the Magic could be proud of their amazing playoff run. They defeated two teams that each had won 60 games during the regular season (Boston, 62 wins; Cleveland, 66 wins). That was the first time that had happened in NBA history. Dwight set an NBA record by posting 22 double-doubles (in 23 games) during the 2009 NBA Playoffs (a double-double is when a player has 10 or more points and 10 or more rebounds in the same game).

"I think we had a great season this year," Dwight said. "We came a long way as a team.

"Our goal was in reach . . . but next year we've got to be even hungrier to want to be champions."